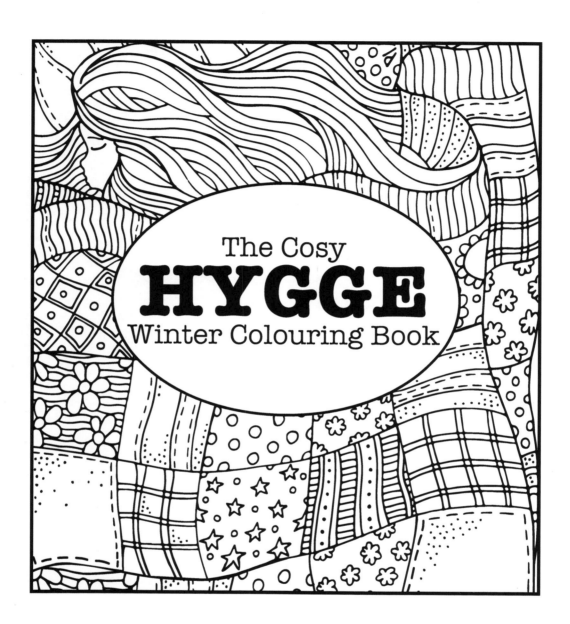

The Cosy HYGGE Winter Colouring Book

Really Relaxing Colouring Book 23

First published in 2016 by Kyle Craig Publishing

Text and illustration copyright © 2016 Kyle Craig Publishing Ltd, Shutterstock Inc.

Editor: Alison McNicol

Cover Design: Julie Anson

ISBN: 978-1-78595-249-4

A CIP record for this book is available from the British Library.

A Kyle Craig Publication

www.kyle-craig.com

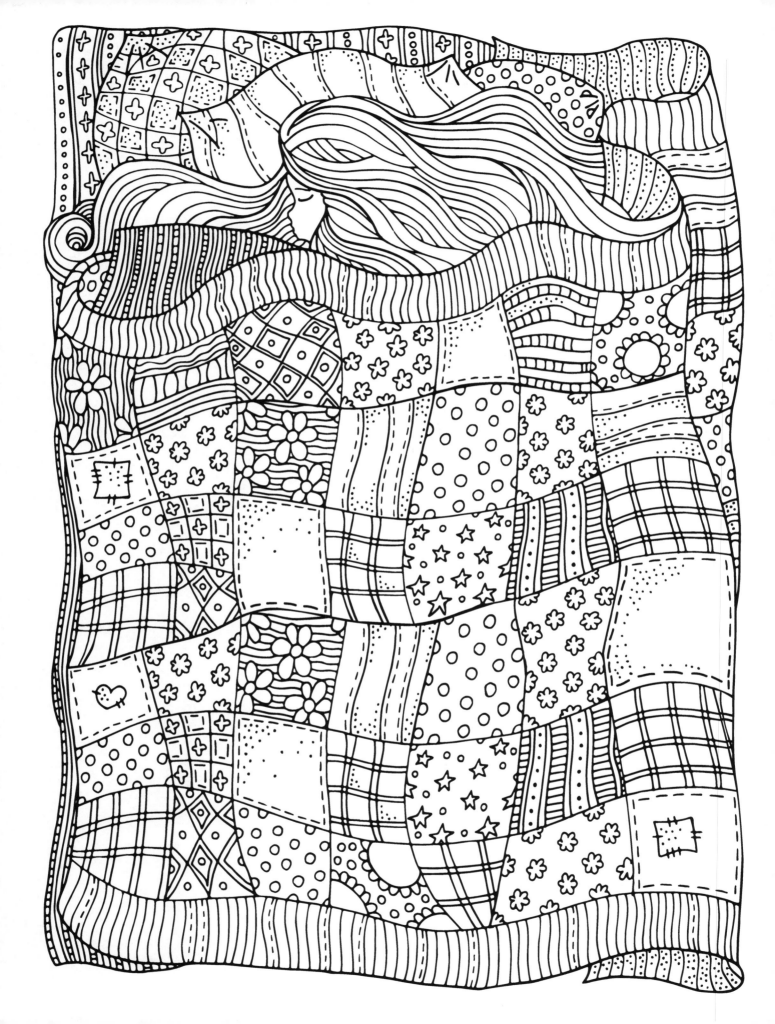

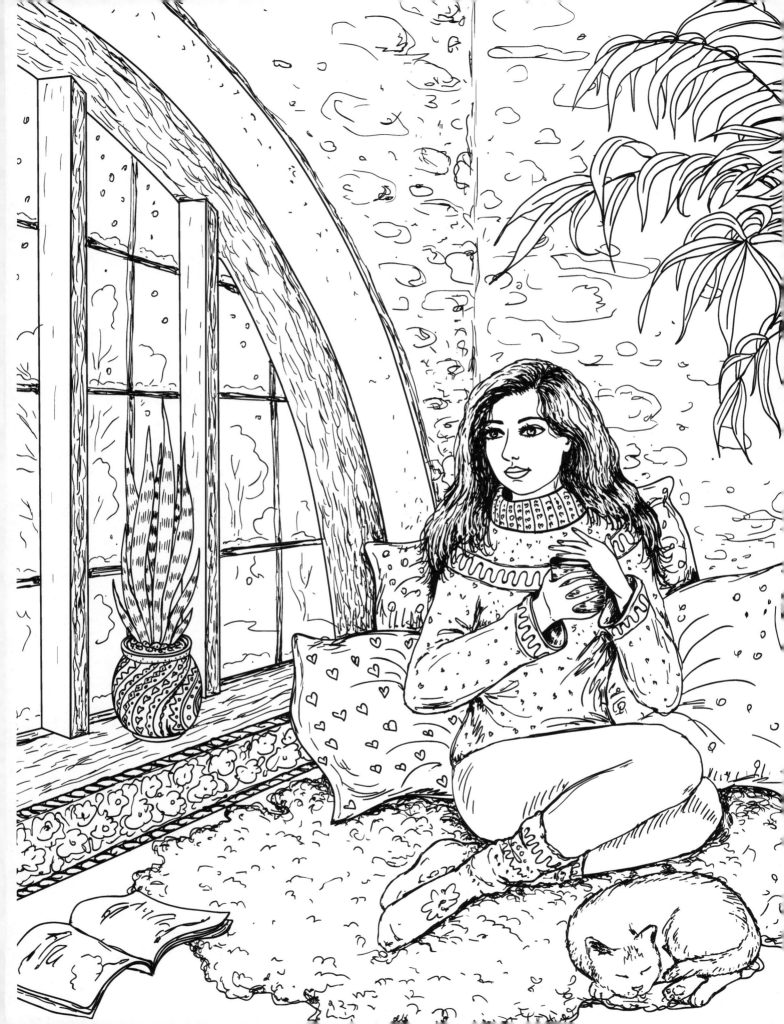

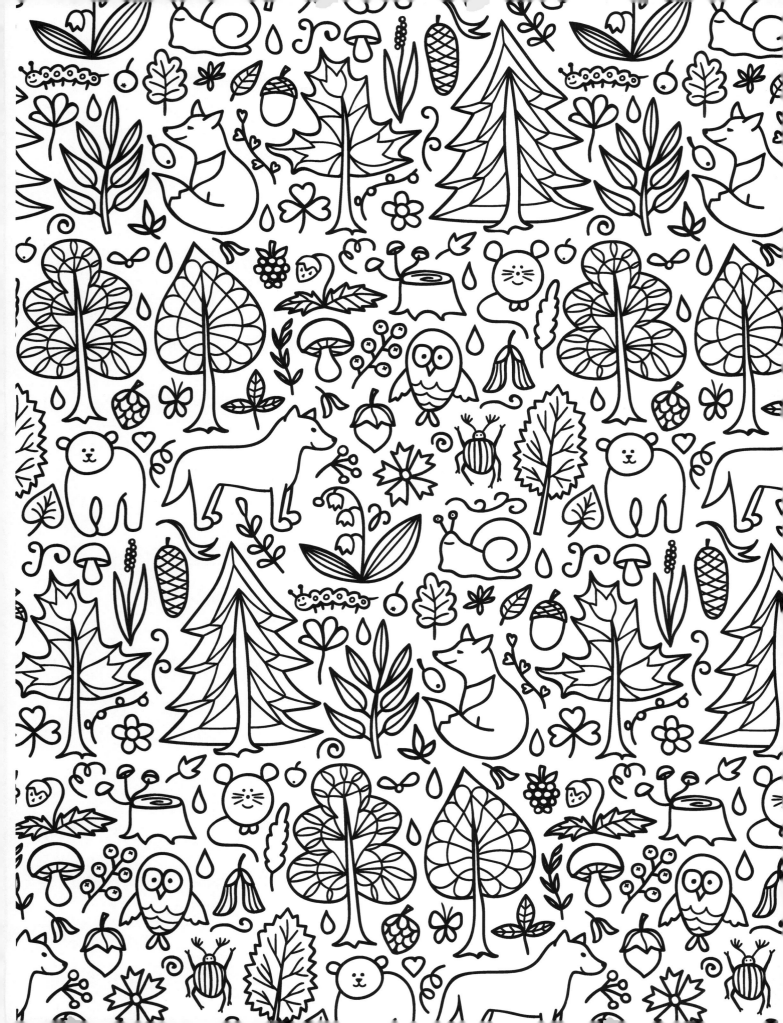

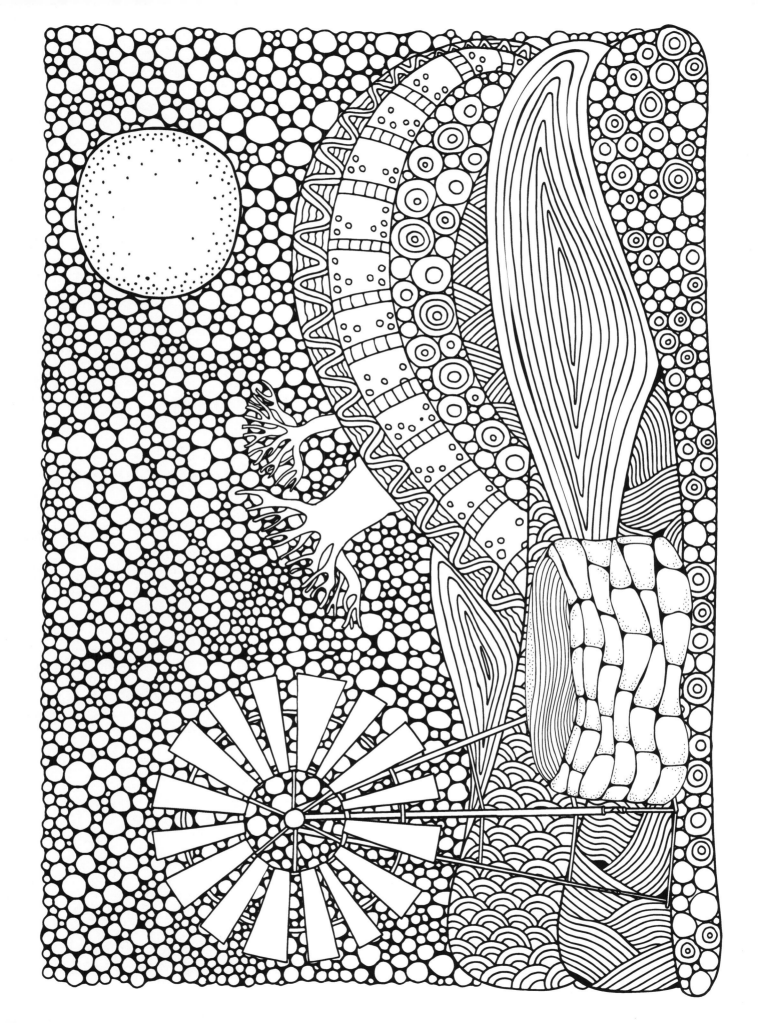

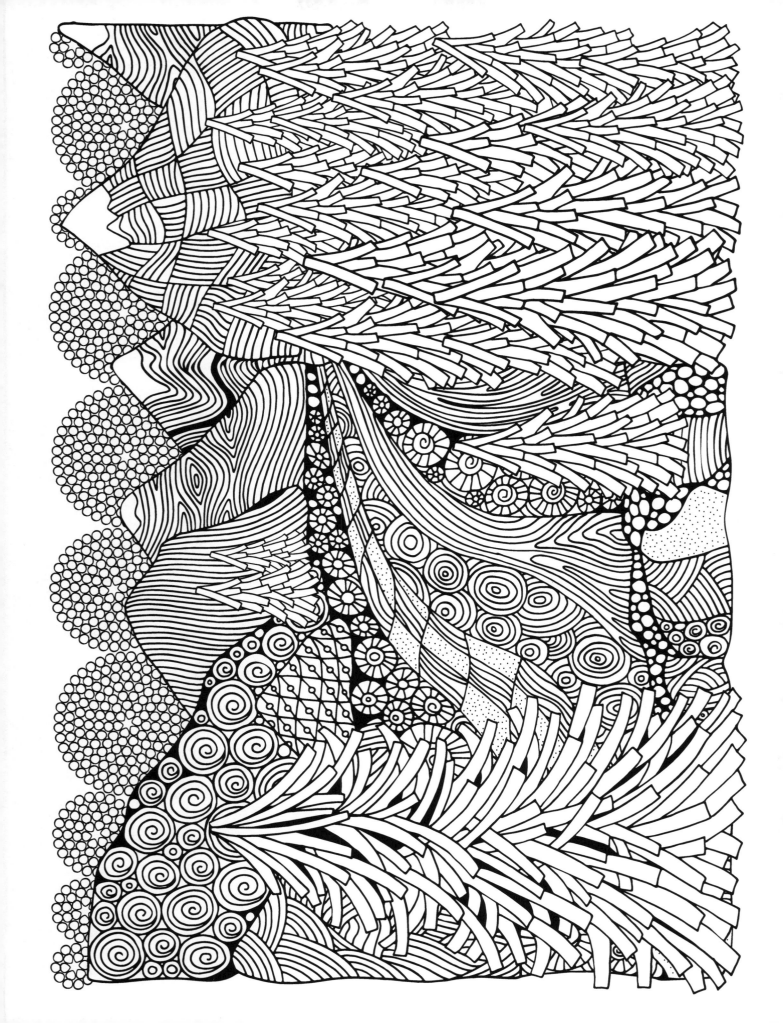

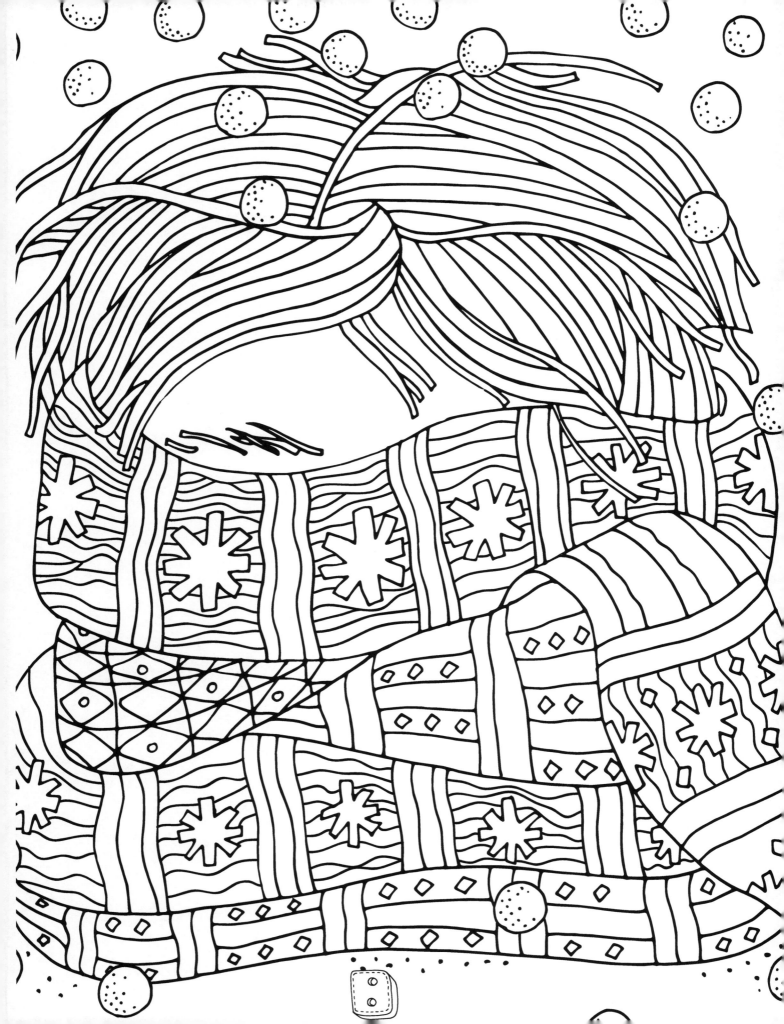

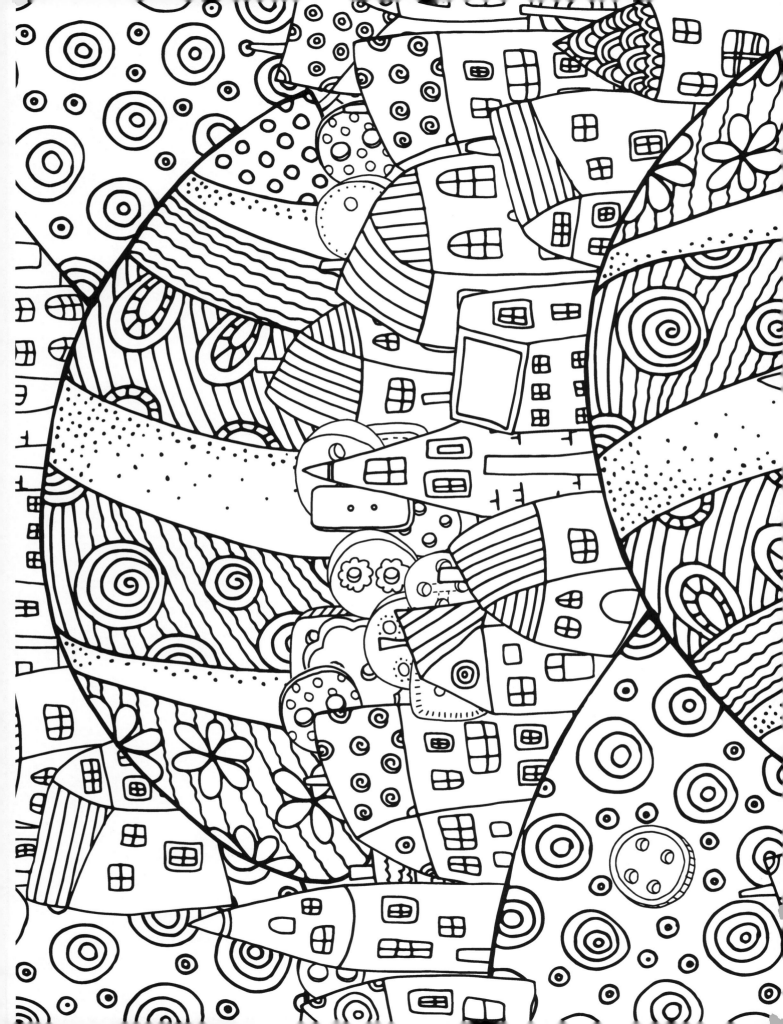

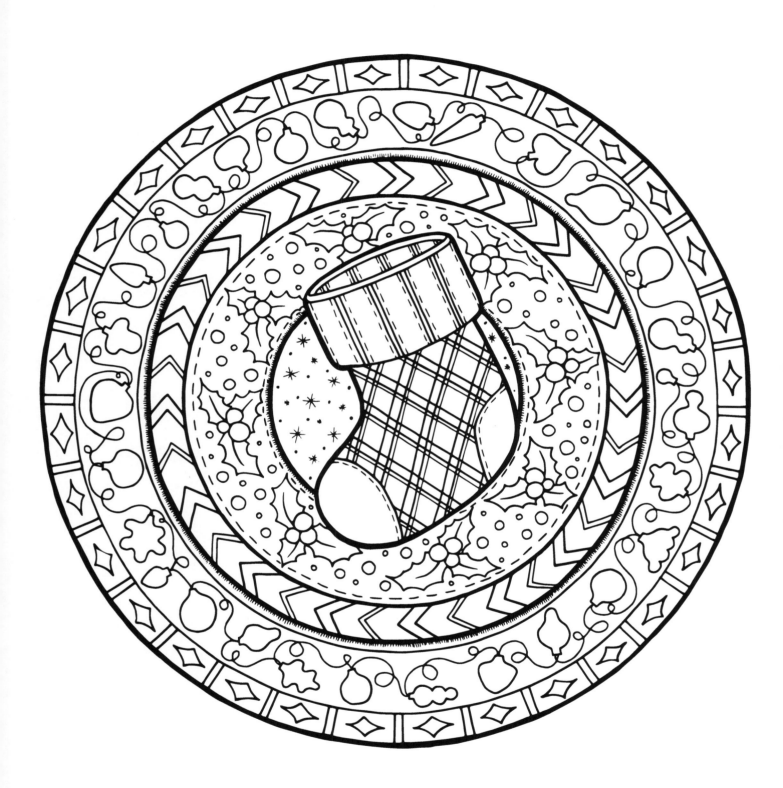

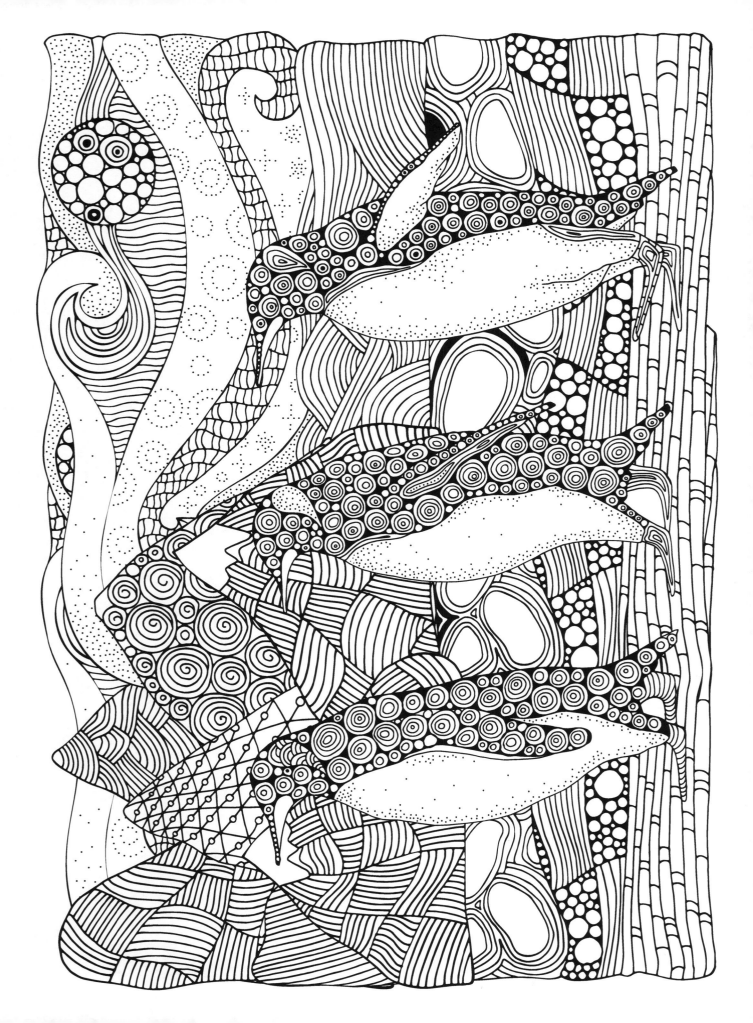

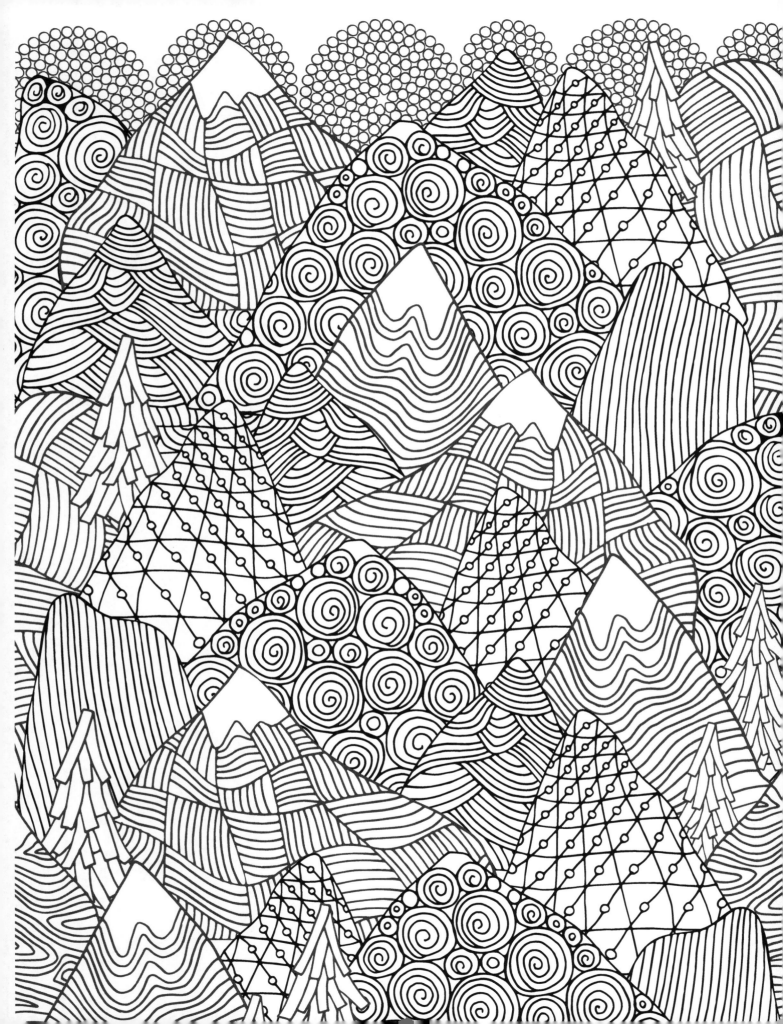

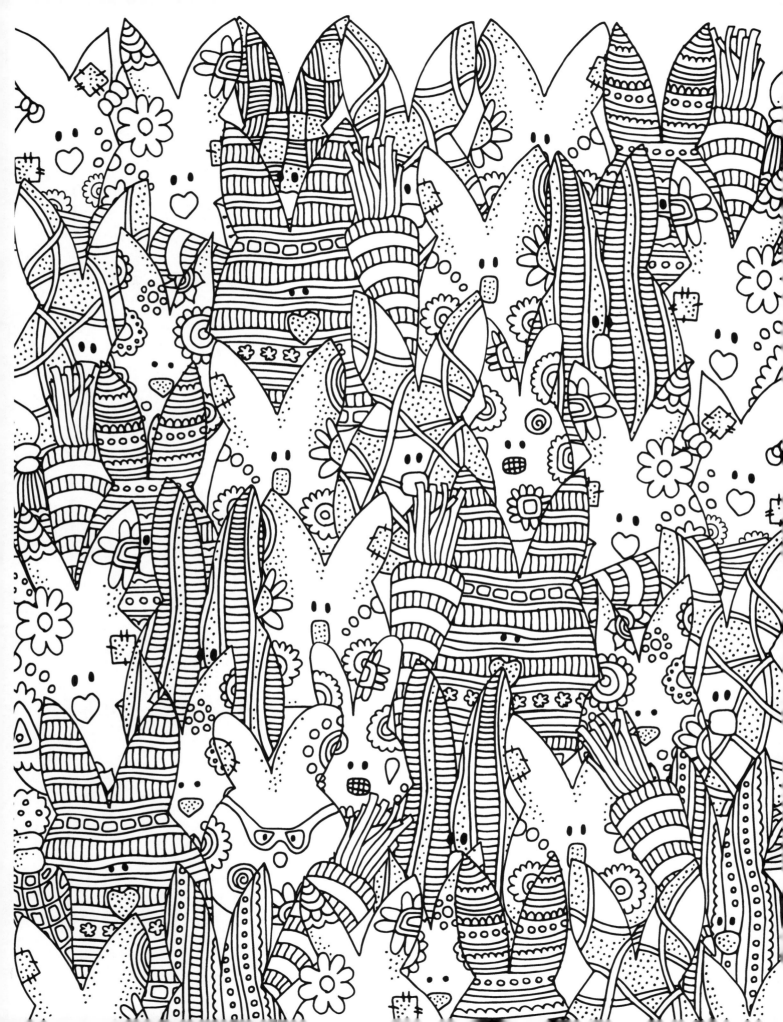

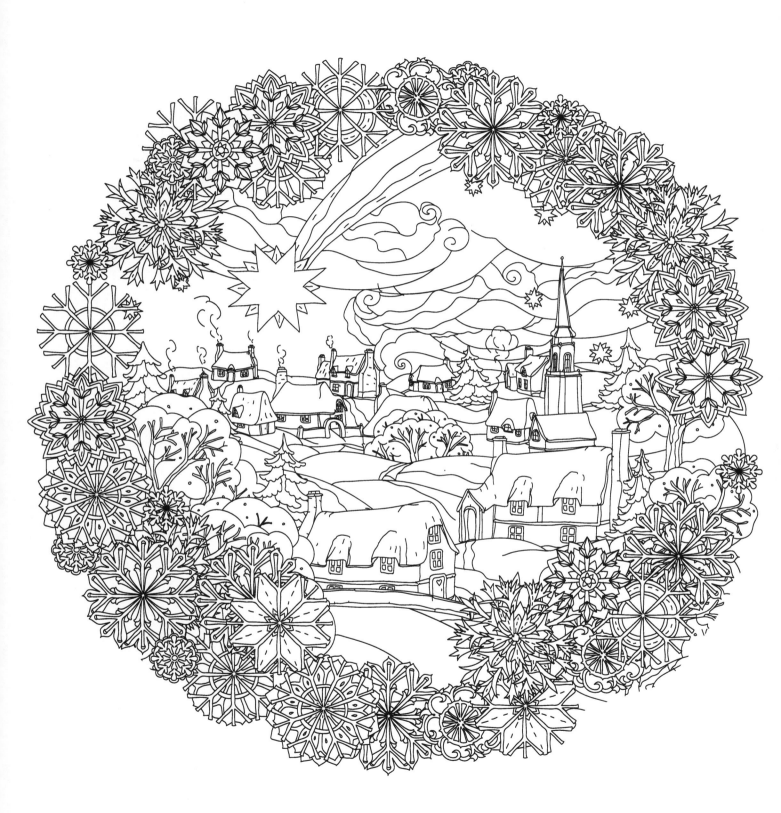

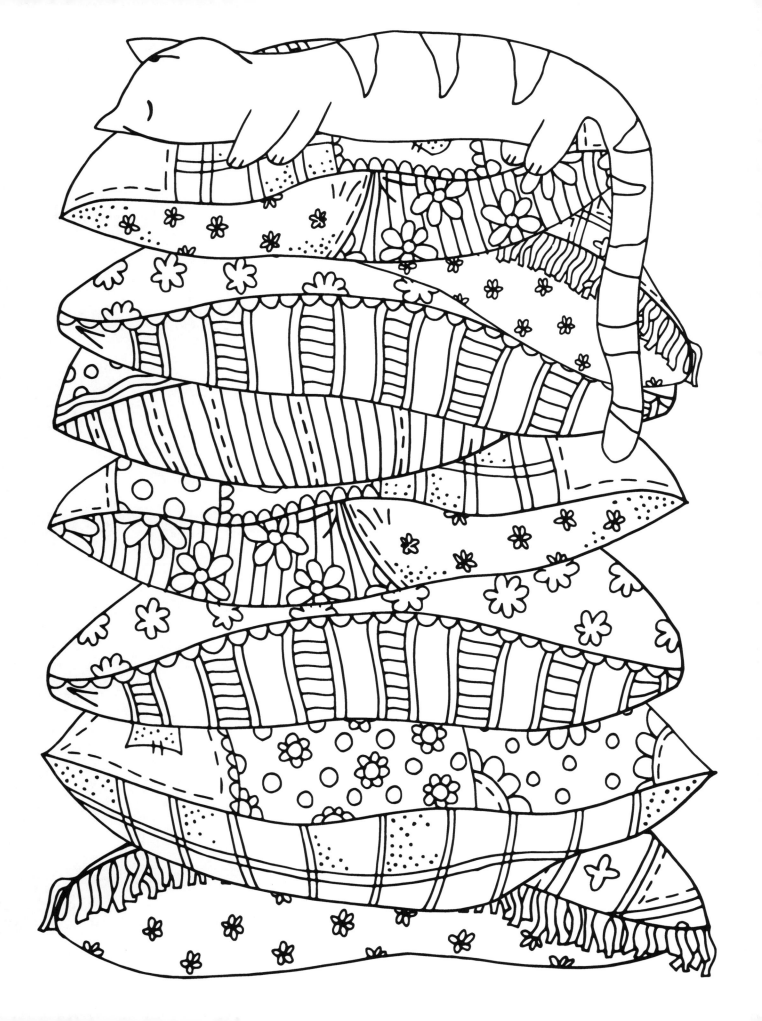

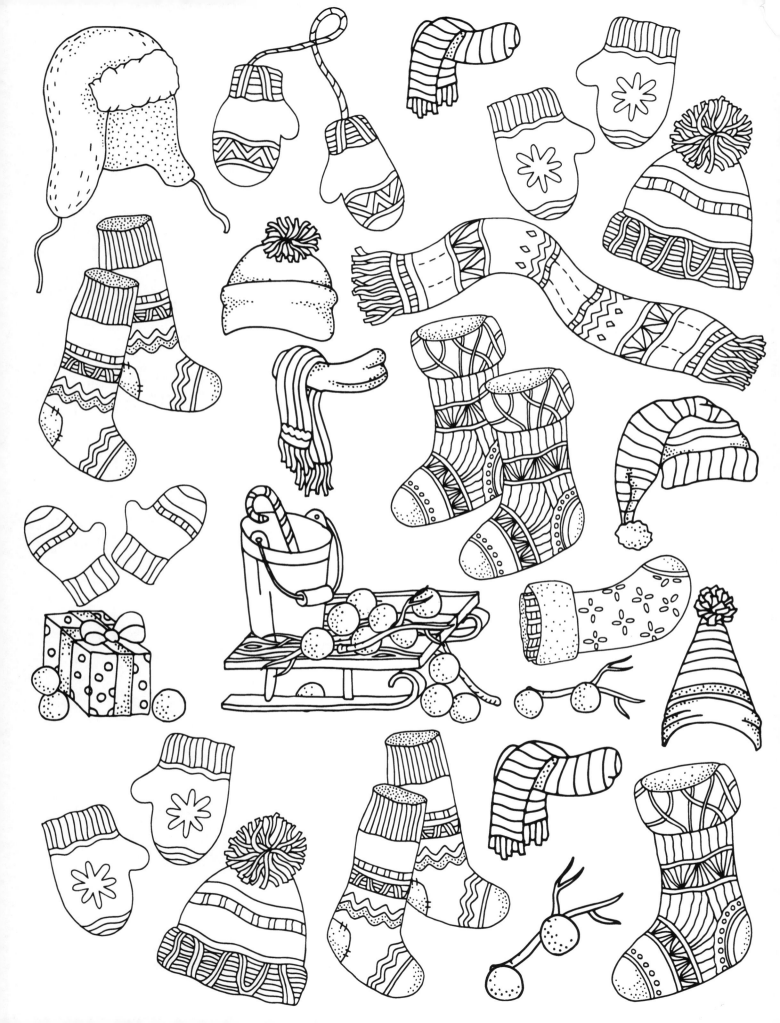

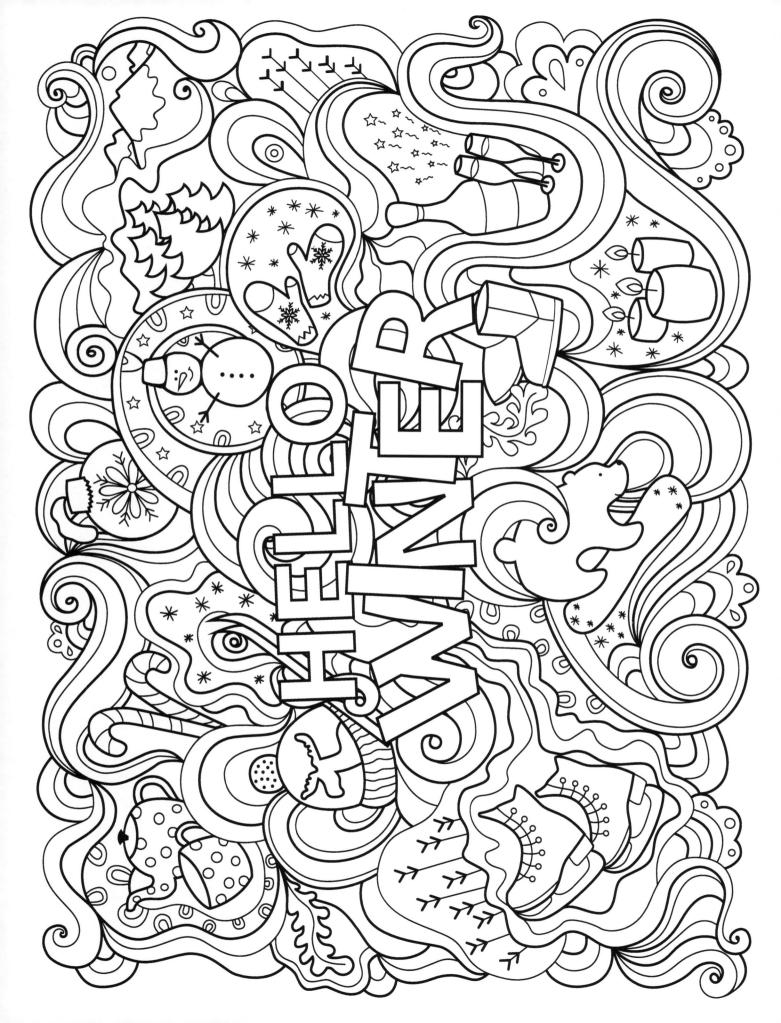

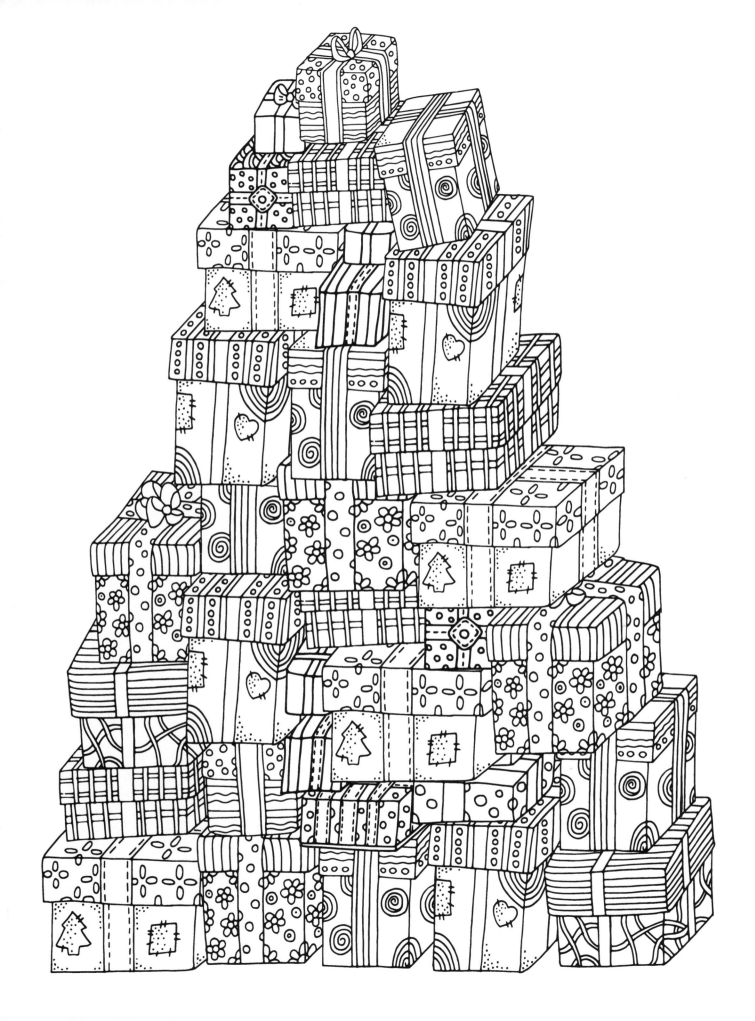

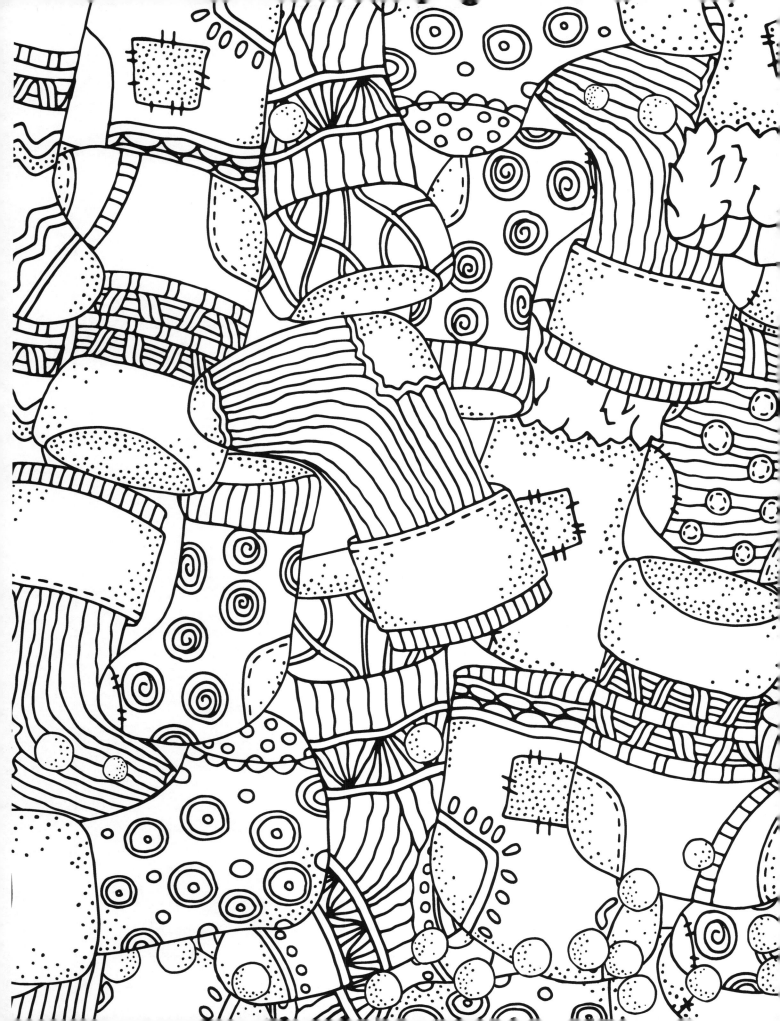

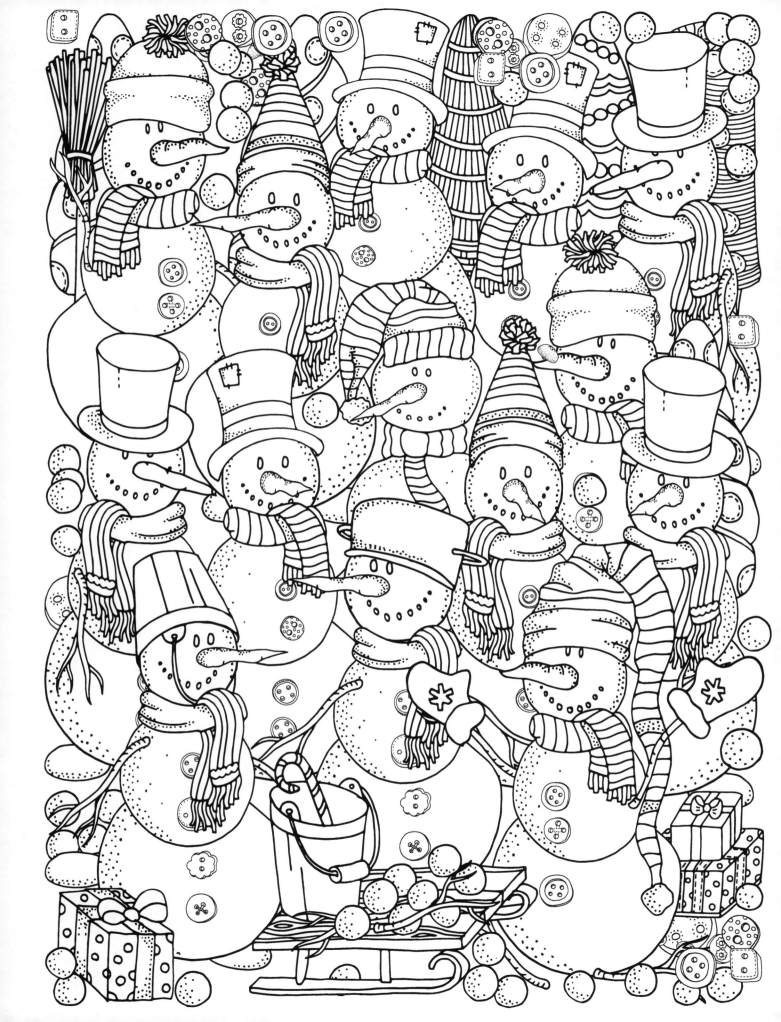

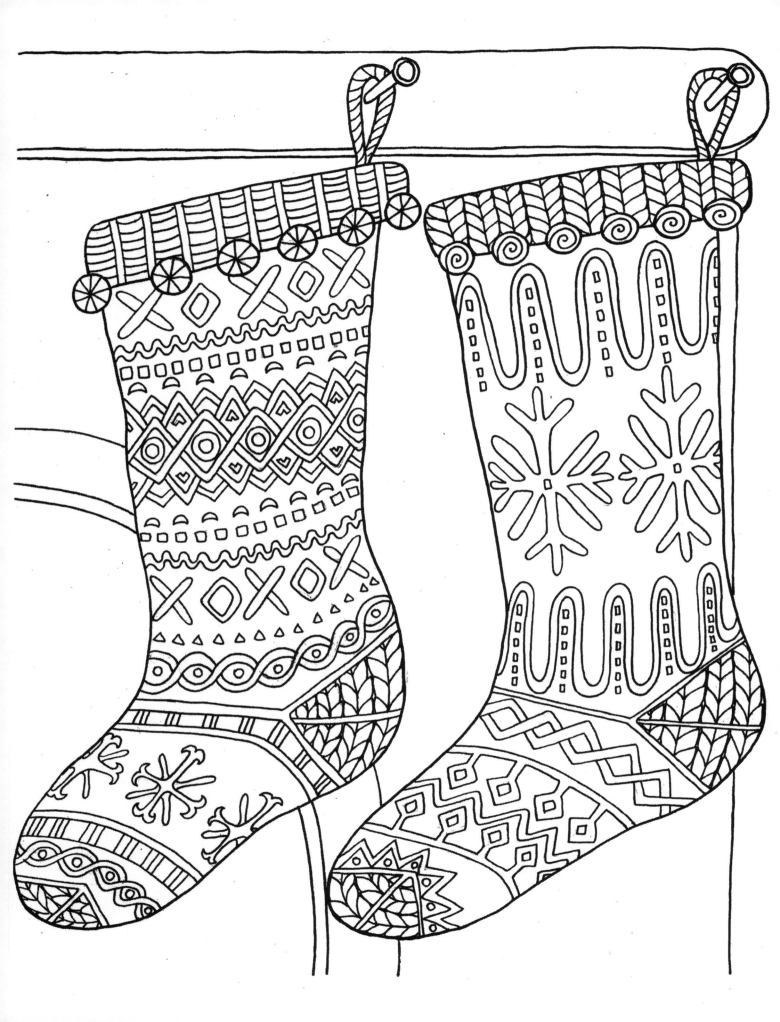

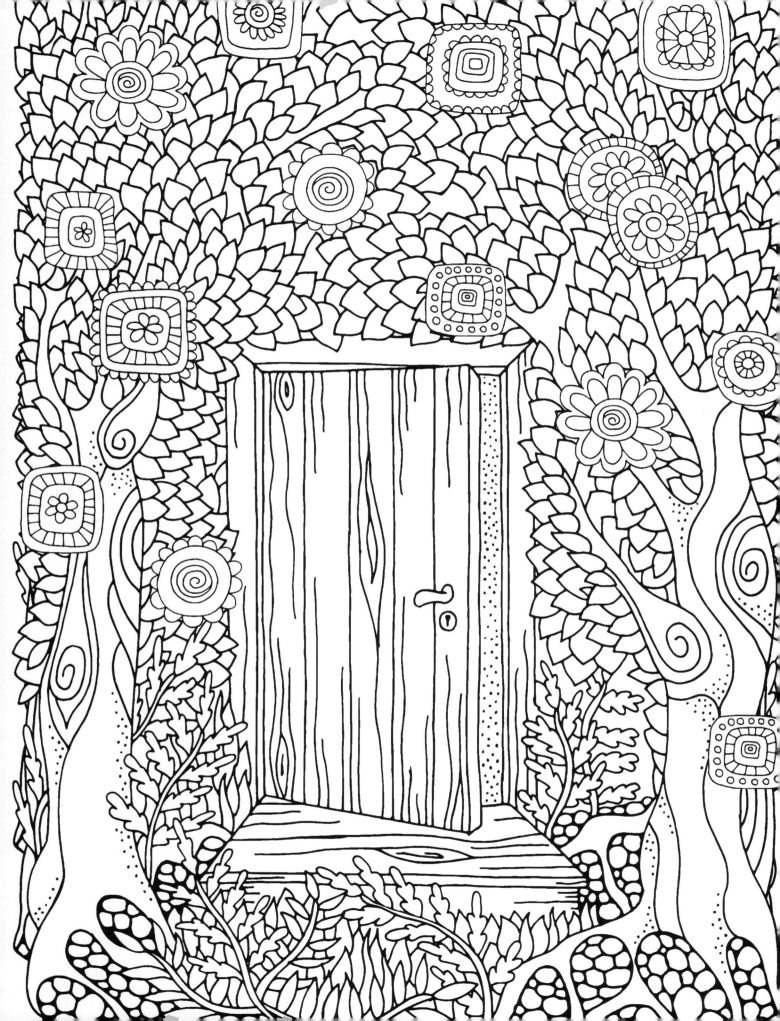

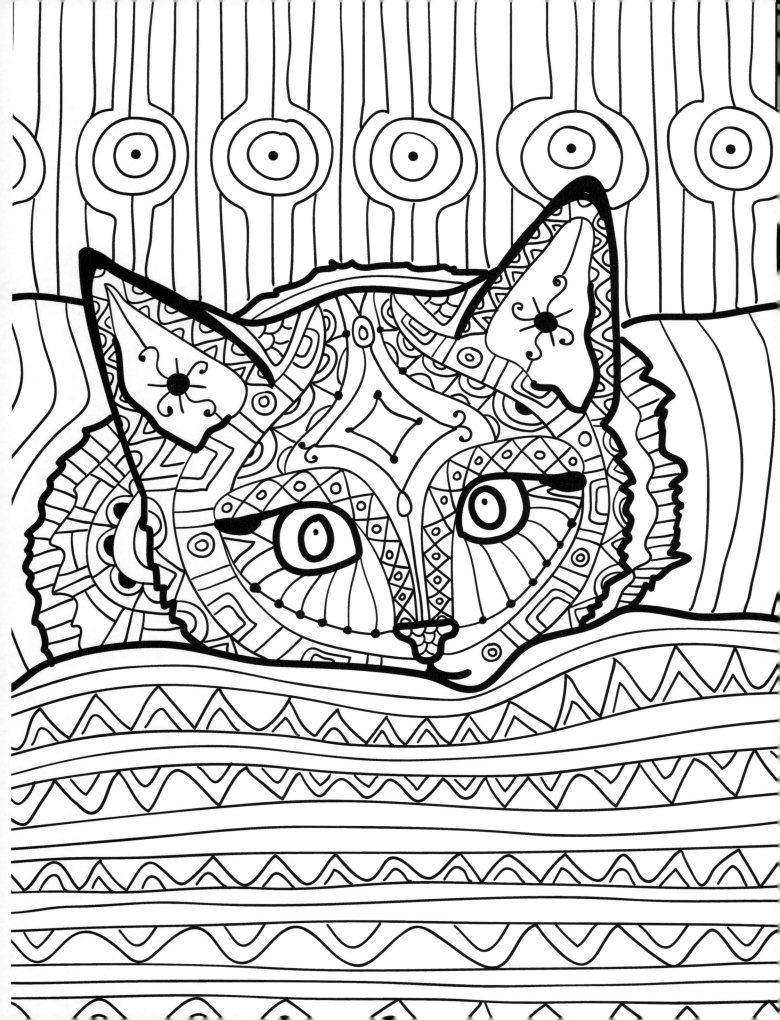

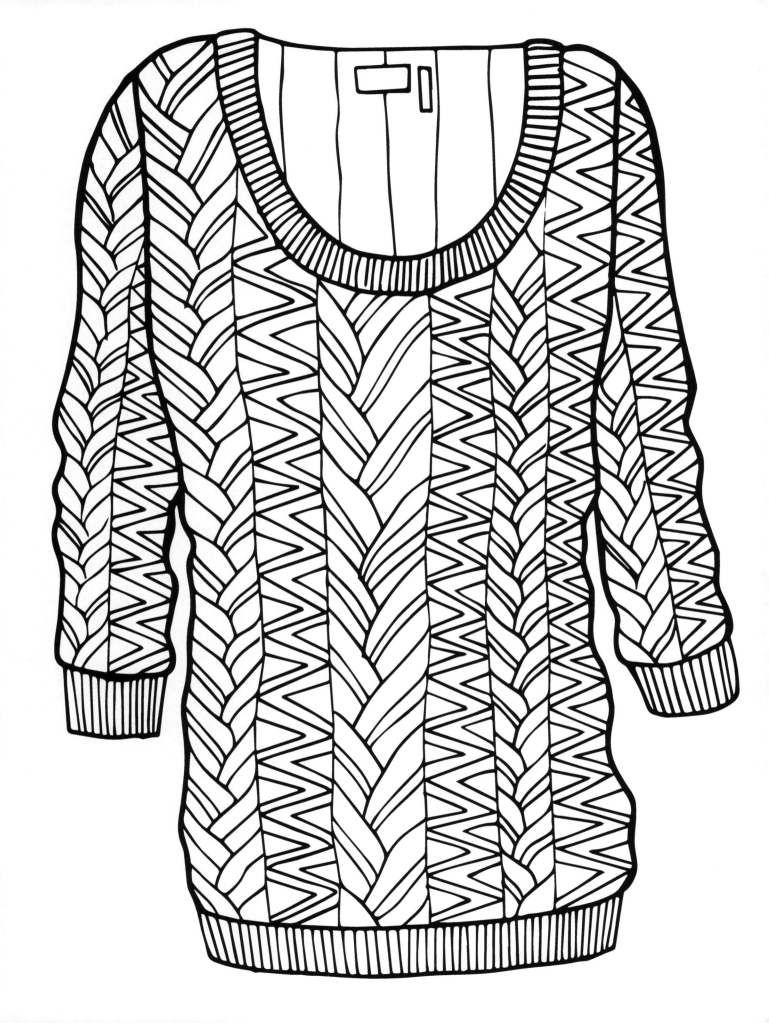

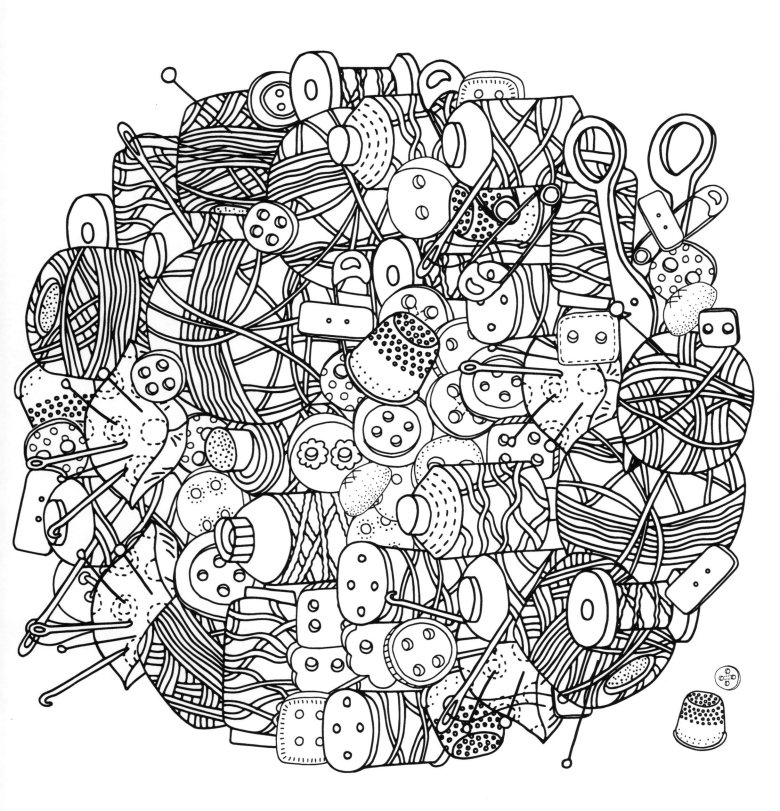

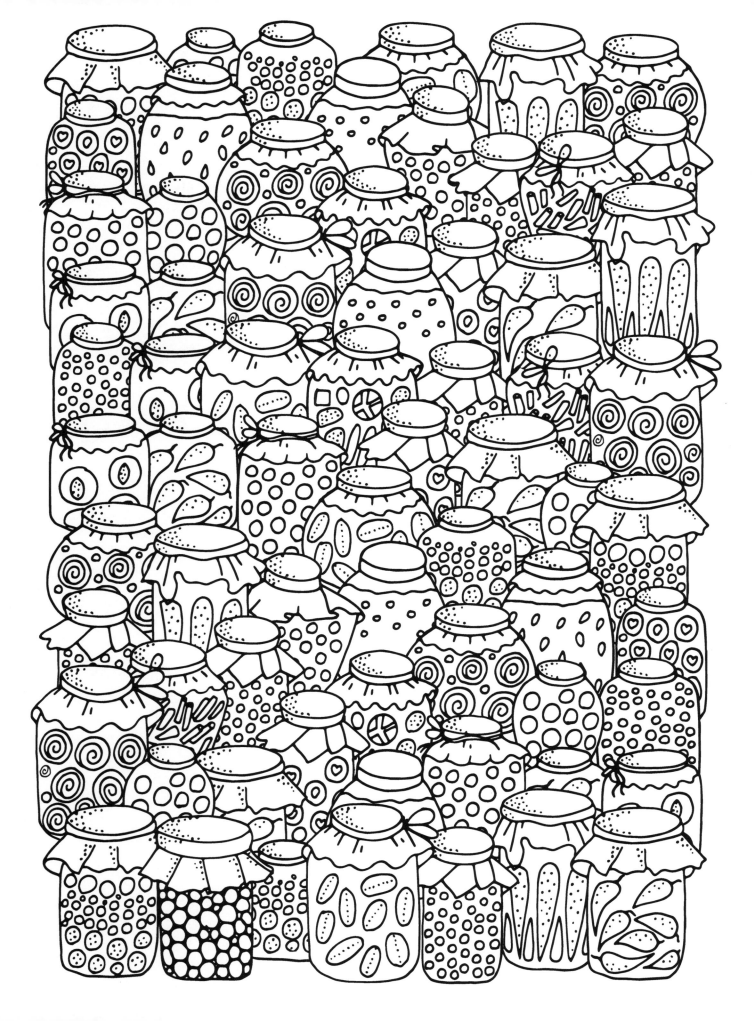

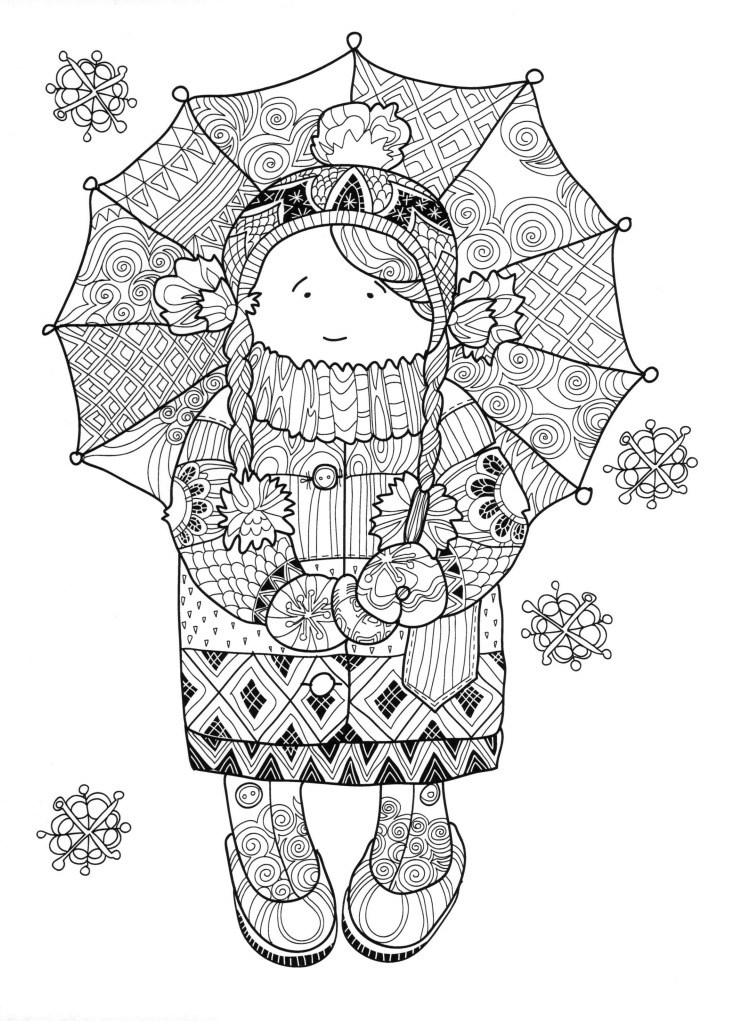

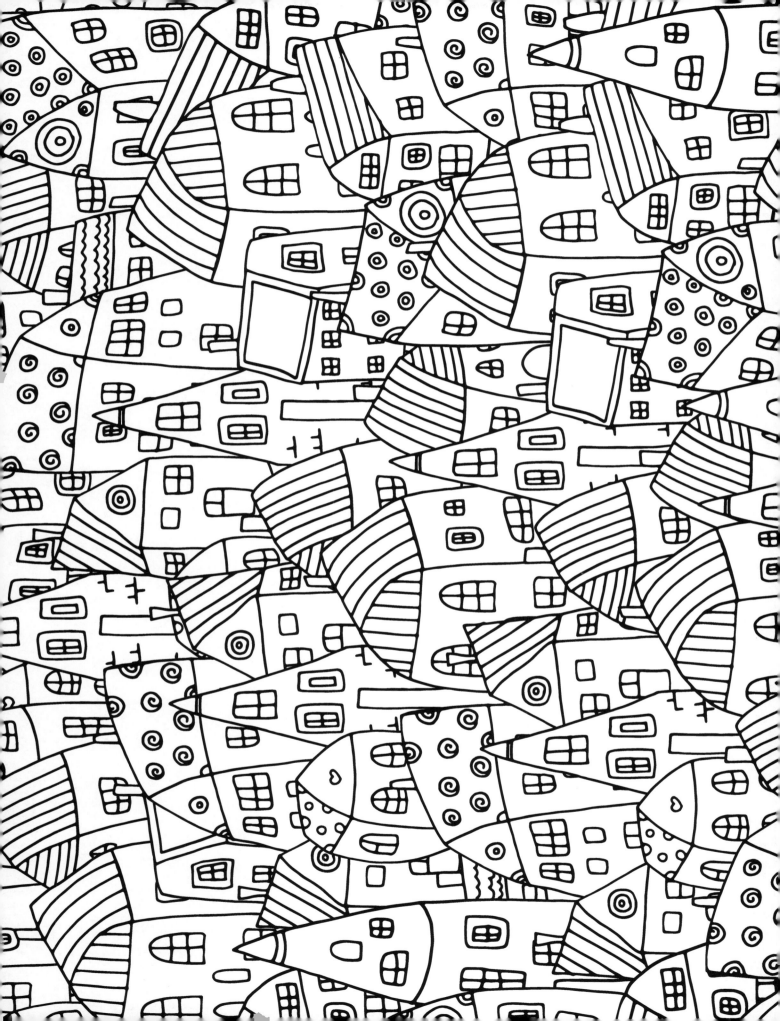

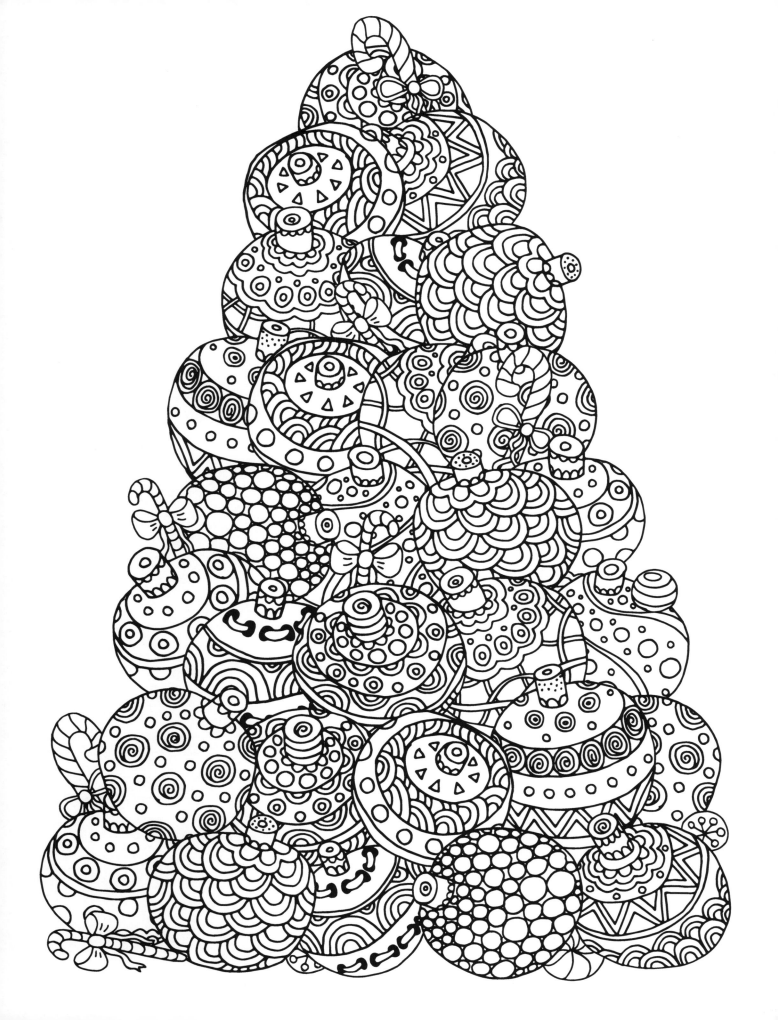

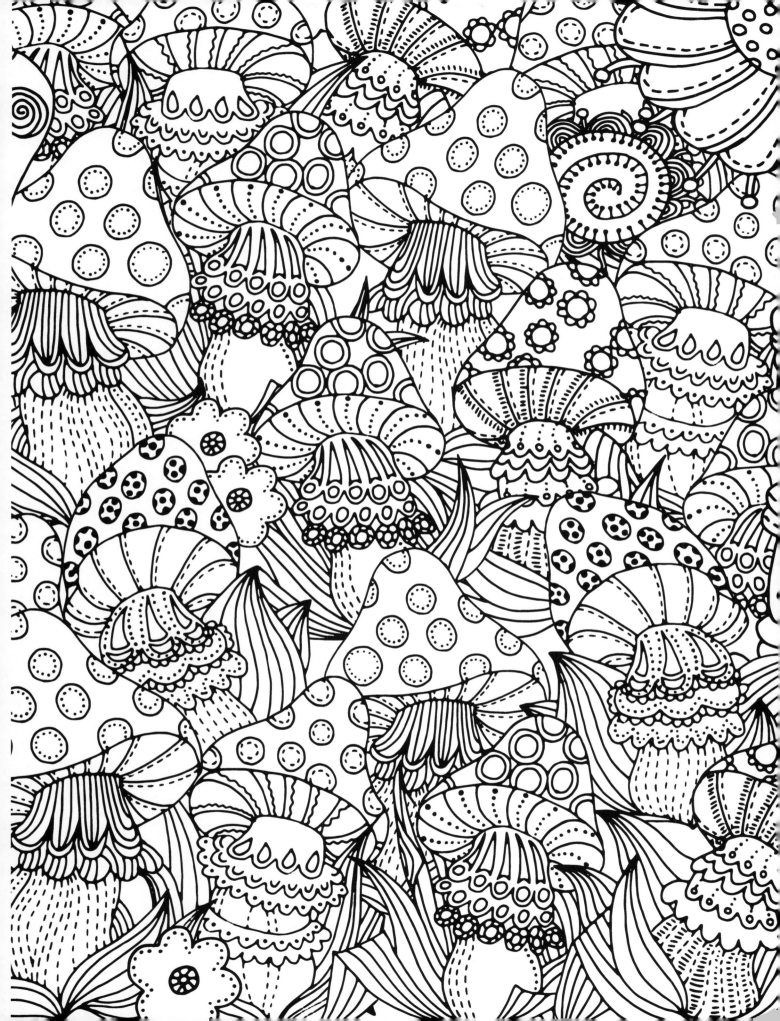

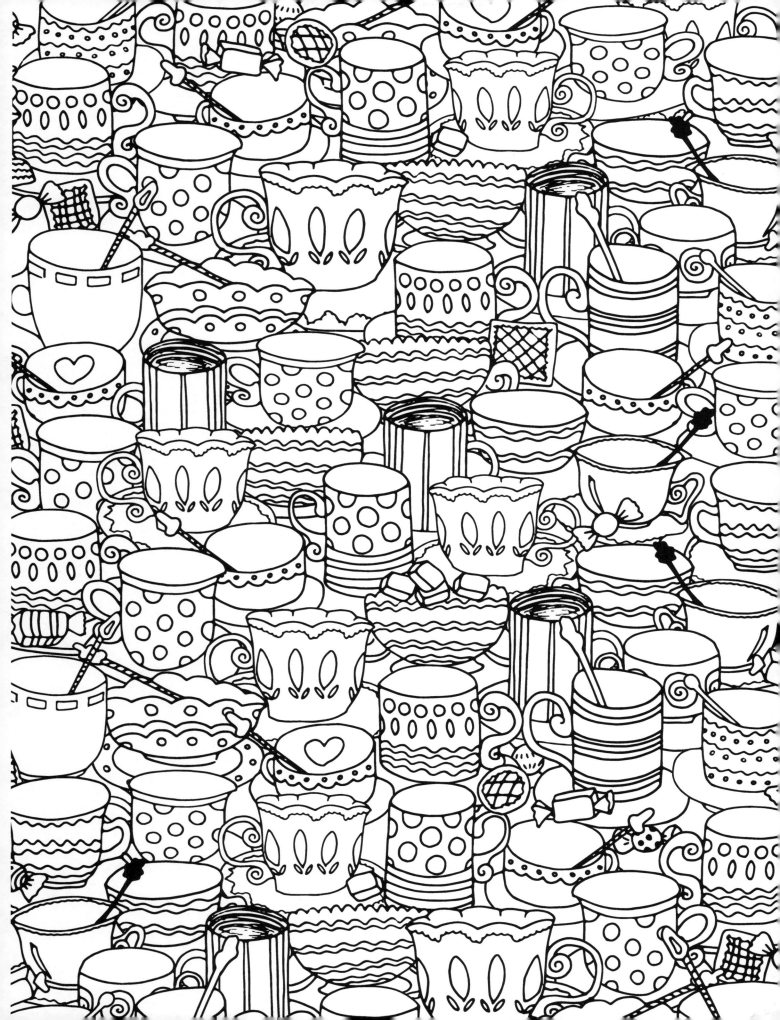

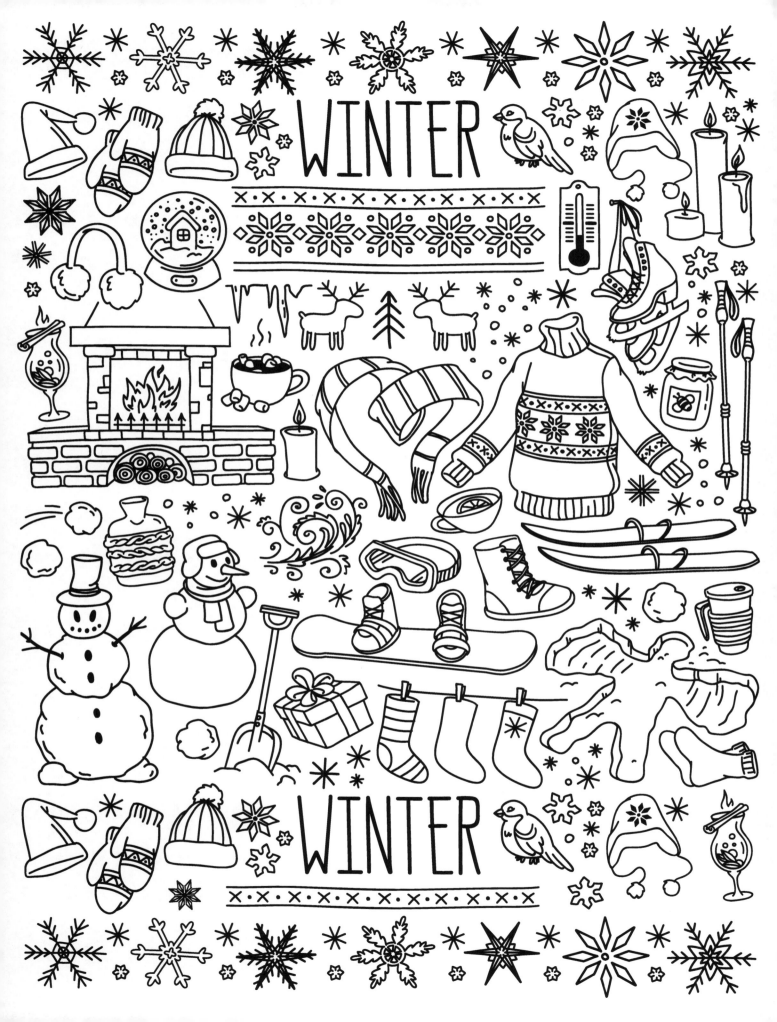

WINTER

WINTER

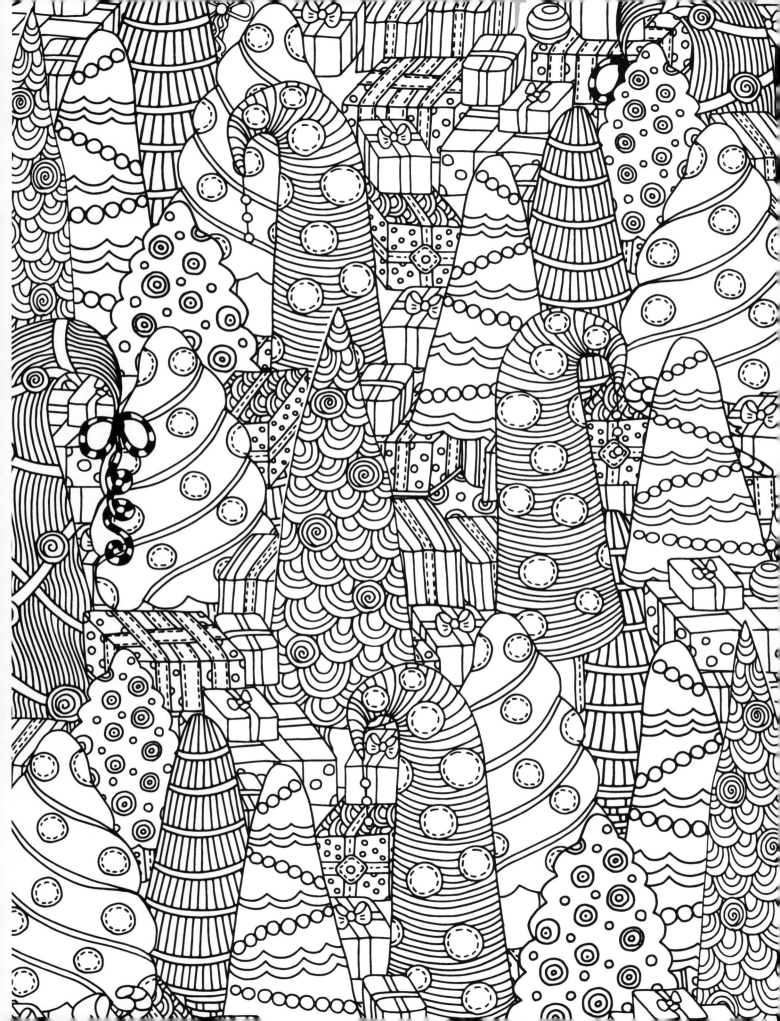

Printed in Great Britain
by Amazon